Point A to Point B

Poems

Michelle Chen

Copyright © 2019 by Michelle Chen

All rights reserved. No part of this book may be reproduced in any manner without written consent except for the quotation of short passages used inside of an article, criticism, or review.

Get Fresh Books, LLC
PO BOX 901
Union, New Jersey 07083

getfreshbooksllc.com

ISBN: 978-0-9989358-8-1
Control Number: email info@getfreshbooksllc.com

Cover image: "post-factual" by Marwa Helal

Cover design & book layout: Ann Davenport

Edited by: Lynne McEniry & Roberto Carlos Garcia

Contents

Avenue	1
Bird-Watching on the Cross-Bronx Expressway	3
A News Cycle	6
Ashore	8
Wrecked	10
The Window	12
Hospice	13
A Place	15
Corkboard	17
Clean Break	19
Traffic	20
Warmest on Record	21
Field Song	22
Help Wanted	24
The Sanctuary	26
Mark	30
Thank You	32
About the Poet	33

Point A to Point B

Avenue

On the northwest corner
things never seemed to turn

The red-striped canopy hung
                                      at an eternal angle
like the second hand on a
watch keeping half
-hearted vigil over
                      the little girl
who scraped her knee
running to the ice cream truck

             to beat the line,
elbowing out
             her neighbors,
clutching damp dollars
in the clamor for soft serve
cones

Sticky soles of a first pair
of heels kissing a
                puddle of spilled soda

Sprung from the bus stop
across the avenue,
to a better part of town
and better beyond
and now
her first visit home

A new clump of cash,
in her pocket a bag
of peppermints for cousins
with names long
          forgot,

reintroducing herself from a
      forgotten age
but old enough to take sweets
from strangers now

Heartbeat quickening
mining memories
for the number of the apartment
door scrawled in magic
marker—not seen since she turned
her head and heard it slam
              right behind
            her

Guessing, she knocks
the door clicks for her

A peephole winks back

Hankering for a different sweetness,
today
a run
trickles down
her stocking,
a streak of silver lines her jaw

Another swing
        hinges
        flails
        twirls
as another girl
flees through
the hall
across the avenue
and away

Bird-Watching on the Cross-Bronx Expressway

Every morning starts in the same place,
with my aunt opening a window
with a duct-taped crack that blooms
in the shape of a dandelion

Climbing the fire escape,
slippers plod to the tar-papered rooftop

Here she keeps
a sanctuary of
two twitching
parakeets suspended
in a rattan dome,
a fat gray pigeon
encased in bent bars,
one empty cage,
dangling, quivering
from the inside
of a stack
of milk crates,
globular rattan bars overlaid
with plastic arabesque

In my mind,
behind closed lids,
I see her playing the roving
bird-watcher
      who never got away

Traipsing up to the roof
while uncle snores below,
ascending to the crisp dawn
leaping across the alley,
ledge
    to ledge,
    bounding over

the expressway to some distant
refuge up north,
landing in damp loamy dirt,
roaming barefoot,
fat toes liberated,
digging into wormholes in the dirt
Feral aunt crouching in the thrush,
gossamer nightgown,
capacious bosom gathered behind
a berry bush

She looks small again
back on her island,
lifts a pair of silver binoculars
over her baggy eyes,
         and listens for the bird calls

None of the din of rushing traffic,
no clanging of the El,
a dawn in
        eternal suspense

Waits for an owl to stir, stalking
Lesser Yellowlegs

Different species of the abandoned,
Wild Tame Migrants all the same
Passing through,
en route to more exotic climes

In my mind she is no longer
stranded on the roof,
        snatching on the precipice
                      of a wild beyond,
but back on terra firma,
admiring the lush migratory flocks,
nesting raptors clustered above,

suspended—untied down,
each element of the scene
ranged around the compass

No passports waived through
with a fold in the corner
on a frayed page of an Audubon guide

On a route old as the seasons,
no boundaries,
no trespass signs marking where
sanctuary begins and ends

I see my aunt in flight
in the morning
before waking downstairs
to discover, a niece estranged
                from a shore never seen,
the inside of a cage left open,
recaptured by an aunt who never flew away

Here, we're kept too—

Only lost birdwatchers here,
ensnared on the wrong side
of an open cage door

A News Cycle

Today a child celebrated her twelfth birthday
behind a barbed wire fence
and remembered seeing her aunt's face
get blown off as she blew the flames out
on each candle of her cake,
save one—

This afternoon thousands of revelers
cascaded onto the street to watch
parade floats roll under fireworks
until they heard the explosions
grow into something more menacing
The Doppler effect of a war
at the bleeding edge of the horizon

Last week's headline in the left margin today
The repetition bores us

Bodies mowed down with strange regularity
A truck with a broken windshield
surges faster than the velocity
of glass shards hitting the pavement

We recognize only later our own street signs
blown back in the lower third on nightly news,
casting shadows over sunny-side up
the next morning

A boy will exhale as he passes through
the metal detector at his school's front door,

then recoil, ashamed the guards heard
the timbre of wheeze exiting his lungs,

not knowing how sharply he'll inhale
as a bullet breaks through the night's hush
to pierce skull before his mind's eye
has a chance to imagine his mother's
scream slamming the walls of the trauma center,
clattering into a chamber of echoes,

ringing down the hospital corridor

Today everything went dark before
the sun rose in other time zones

We can check the weather in every capital
before flipping the channel for a nature documentary
on antimatter and the law of gravity

Each force has its equal opposite force,

each tragedy, a historical counterweight

We pray for time to pass before there's a chance
we might ask the wrong questions

Ashore

The island sprawls—
A drop of blood unfurls,
ripples forth onto azure tides

A crystalline froth buoys the elements
of a sacrifice—the tiny fingers on the horizon,
the soft ribs exposed under the cinch
of an orange foam vest,
pinched in pain—bobbing in vain

A futile vessel carries the wreck of a family tree

Branches calcified into balsa wood,
jostling bones— fresh marrow nibbled by fish
tangled in the rot of a hungry world

Their rattle keeps us writhing and grasping
Rasping hearts beat, babies bleat
for another day, a new pulse

People of a different shore bear the weight
of another history of conquest after conquest

A Trojan king, a Persian emperor,
occupations, colonies, assault, retreat, surrender
And still they come, iridescent bodies flailed
on an altar bearing scraps of children encased in jewels
imprisoned in the original sin of exile

A salty sea peppered with cages,
honeycombs of purgatory
stranded at high tide, a strayed vessel

This island bleeds—

Carrion lies astride the shore,
where the world comes to slake a thirst,
parched by dispossession

In those cracking rubber dinghies
with sun-bleached streaks,
tattered emblems,
washed clean of allegiances

The ocean touches this shore,
the first and last kiss of a refugee's afterlife
The rotting debris on this voyage is immaterial
Paradise floats just beyond the sightline

Here a wreath lies, betrays a torn hull
Here an ocean of engorged barbarity laps
at the sand, flushes away tufts of fine hair,
burnt flannel, a pink wool sock, a surfaced shell

A lucid dream that never wakes
trails a wake that never ends

Wrecked

The last thing he held was his son's left hand
as the waves closed in, the clasped fingers of
sea foam tightening eddies around their small ears,
their flared nostrils trembling above the rising tide

Blood seeped from under his salted irises,
the turgid lids lulling heavy as the boat
he was trying to carry on one buckled shoulder,
his boys clutching the other

Tiny palms braced, fell limp,
or was that his grip going limp,
even as he felt his balled fist harden
like a mercury drop—heavier than the sea

Somewhere between those surfaces,
tensions weakened, the grip gave way
to a force calling him home

Just a mile offshore,
a father began his homecoming that day,
an open palm unfurling alongside
a child's calcified fist

Here the earth,
not the water—lies between

The father once led the boy away,
now follows him home,
buoying him, on his shoulder

Again, both pairs of eyes sealed
with the acid balm of saltwater

He still floats above his son, unable to sink further,

though he still tries now, his ear to the soft mound,
cradling the grave—the surface impregnable

Though he listens still for a breath he can salvage
and hold above this place—he stays mired where he belongs

The Window

It seems mandatory
to install a small window
         in every prison cell

Placed perfectly at the line of sight
just skirting the prisoner's forehead
Brushes the day's edge just so,
admitting a slanted sliver of daylight,
the horizon
         just beyond

Forever dusk—forever dawn,
never shadow
         only a tempting snatch of sky

A periscope missing the last mirror
A perspective that taunts and teases,
         waves the scent of the sun
without its warmth

An echo of
         an echo of words never heard

Half blindness—neither here
         nor there

The prisoner imagines planets
orbiting the cell spinning on its axis,
wrapping gravity ever tighter around
madness filling the corners where absence
dwells

Hospice

Now that you're almost gone,
I can hold your hand,
know how deeply to press
my thumb in your palm,
feel the pressure point,
how far to pull your wrist,
knead through your doughy clasp,
coil my stare 'round the ticking
clock behind you

Now that you're fading,
you surface in sharp relief

The backdrop is a mildew watermark
blooming through the wallpaper,
the abandoned breakfast tray
on the nightstand scatters
a constellation of yellow crumbs
in the foreground snowing on false ivy

Pools of light over the shadowed lakes,
tightened into angry puddles

The tides gather as plaintive ripples,
Sisyphean boulders that hammered
the roof now pounded into
                        skipping
                                    stones

Within reach, elbow-deep,
in those organs where secret debts
burrow into your kidneys,
nestle in the crook of your neck,
in the seam between my fingers—your shoulder

A ragged gown, crepe crown, diaphanous
wing draped over shriveled knees

Halfway gone, an aperture opened in your mind,
under the sterile lights of the hospice,
a final grip—wanted something

A Place

The knock on the door gave her a start,
memory jolting back to the day
when the sun came in from
the opposite side and shadows leaned
the other way

Grass blades leaned lazily,
limp from the heat,
coiling into a gnarled jungle

And a figure slipped from shadow
into dappled light, the freckles glowed embers
into a face curled around a smile
asking if that old lawnmower
in the corner still worked

New in town—needed a place to live,
a job to do

So began twenty years of living,
of doing, staying, never leaving,
and then slowing to a crawl

And then finally a brake,
an abrupt halt on a long accidental trip,
together interrupted by a shift in gears
from night to day

Now dusk was settling in the haze of a life
lived briefly in the daylight,
retreating to darkness,
curdling into memory
before it was ready for recollection

Something called him from somewhere else

The knock came again like an echo
long delayed as the freckles
fade back into the sunset

Almost hearing him say again,
"I'm looking for a place to live"

And wondering what I'm going to do

Corkboard

A graveyard hangs above my desk
plastered with pastel sticky notes,
a corkboard pocked with thumb tacks,
pinned prayer rugs and other ephemera
gathered on past travels

Dust-caked strip mall photo booth portraits,
stacked grins crack into a stuck out tongue

Milky clouded Polaroid frames
ruptured by a rainbow leak

A galactic burn streaks into
a far-flung cloudburst,
a bleeding watermark

The water line stain creeps
through decayed cork clotted,
bled off the edge where
the flood line peaked

Where the last surge of the storm lifted
the rust off steel file cabinets overgrown
with blisters of algae—floating mold lilies

This was a basement,
the foundation of a house,
where crooked picture frames
bow to a splintered Ping-Pong table
adrift, bouncing between the edges
of a flood, throwing up a constellation
of forgotten heirlooms

A stack of drawers that refuse to close,
overstuffed with Mom's bric-a-brac

scrapbooks, glue sticks, pieced-together
tatters of a middle-class household,
the clipped banter, peals of laughter
suspended in childish memory

Browned doilies caked in rot, coiled in
bristly balls of twine, the bits and bobs
of cardboard salvaged from the trash,
a collage of patched memories

The bottom drawer, slack, unhinged,
crusted with barnacles of rust

I don't open it

There lies Mom's banished craft box,
the little rubber stamps, bunnies and tulips,
a taxonomy of fossilized scenes
of campers parked under Wyoming sunsets,

Too many stacks to count,
a frustrated dam of memories impossible
to pull apart

A family album swings in the breeze,
hanging from a rusty thumbtack

Here lies home

Clean Break

The day you left,
I didn't really see you go,
just the wet footprint trailing
from the shower through the lobby,
out the door, into a curtain of light
so sharp it cut the horizon in two

Your matted hair still sticky
with drops of lather, you stormed out,
leaving a faint trail—dramatic silhouette
scrubbed raw, the frayed towel dropped
on hot asphalt—dirty again and shameless

Another clean break from all the things
I can't wash my hands of, looking down
at grimy footprints, on slippery tiles,
wondering how to explain this to the neighbors

Traffic

The light turns green and we are told to go,
that it is safe to turn ourselves

The day she turned thirteen she learned
not to look both ways—she forgot when to go
(another way of saying
                        forgot when to stop)

Learned how to turn other heads,
tugging the edge of her cotton shirt down
when the summer breeze brushed past,
pointing down and up at the same time

Flash of a damp midriff signals traffic,
halts breath, yields a sigh,
wheels heave—traffic dances
the intersection out of syncopation

The day she turned thirteen,
traffic started to move in a different direction,
light veered in from different angles,
summer breeze blurred—a propulsion lurched,
throttled a hot grate into the blinking arrow

And when it hit her, ignited a flame,
a burning tire rolling around
the crosswalk, flames licking
the edge of a steaming gutter

The smoke curled around the manhole lid

                    (festooned with a dirty rose bed)

that hides and tricks the roundabout

Warmest on Record

The warmest winter leaves the heart
in a slump, lungs puckered,
stinking of laundry left in a dryer unspun

Walking through the holiday flea market
at Union Square, adrift among
wreaths of parched pine, wilted orchids,
a season overstayed its welcome

A glistening slick on the sidewalk
kissing my heels reminds me of melted
candy canes, half solid Sno-cones,
bruised brown pears out of season

Floating through the flea market abuzz
with fruit flies—invisible until trapped
in a glass jar, multiplying in the residue
of another insect's nectar

Air too ripe—the mercury drops
below the meridian soft, rotten,
turning to a wine with off notes
of a swelling menace

Field Song

The day his daughter was born
the men's feet began to pad the land,
the plows began to gnash the dirt,
and the birds vanished

Men washed into the pockets of earth
hollowed out by fugitive birds,
summer lull hung in thin, ropy strands,

Limp tongues of a scarecrow's tattered shirt
beat off-key against the whistling winds

Gnarled fists clung to dirt to keep
from getting
                      carried away
                      on the wind

The men picked orange trees as a busker plucks
the strings of a lute, strum the grooves
of a wheelbarrow trail

But silence hovers in the minor key of dusk,
calloused songs braided into wire carrying
dreams home on something not quite wind,
on a sound not quite a lullaby

                                    What time is it there?

The day his daughter was born he began trusting her
to sing herself to sleep, just as she was born trusting
the faraway man, strumming the timbre
of a reedy southern wind

He'll travel in the other direction for a few seasons
till the oranges are left to rot off the tree

and patter the ground in a muted staccato

The rhythm of an over-extended family
stretched over a measure of a long stave

A girl's voice peals somewhere, sweetened
in a man's harvest of welled silence,
waiting for a time to sigh

Help Wanted

A hand scrawled piece of paper
taped to the inside of a plate glass
window in a corner diner

"Help Wanted: Part-Time Dishwasher"
reflected over a magic marker squiggle
of marine blue:

Se Necesita Lava platos … tiempo parcial

The sign speaks two languages,
the broken Spanish shouted from a boss's lips,
the body language of flailing arms strafed
with scalding steam—spattering grease

The musky crush of a clutch of dollar bills
in dawn air skulking out the back entrance
after a night flooded with alien voices rushing
the ears, a swarm of wasps breaking the surface,
allergic to the soap, bleaches out wet babble,
drools Hollandaise, cracked porcelain teeters
in impossible stacks, dangles in the clutch
between chaos and boredom

The language of knowing how to count the bills,
how fast to go, when not to stop,
how to add ten and twelve

All the words you need to survive
another night—to slip through the exit
unnoticed

The door slams behind you,
Medio tiempo means:
eager to let you in

and send you home
without a word

The Sanctuary

Click

The last night in his country,
death squads embraced his sister's wrists
in steel rings

He watched from the cobwebbed crack
that spiraled from the hole in their only window,
patched with the last scrap of black electrical tape

He cursed himself for wasting that final strip
to splay over naked fate, glaring and inescapable

Why even bother to hold the window intact,
as if defying gravity could deny bullets

(They would later need the same tape to bind
red-stained gauze, patching a hole
in the eye of a neighbor's grandchild)

Tape can't piece back together bits and pieces
of beautiful ruins left in a looted home

The mosaic of shards turning sun to moon

The same moon splitting the beam
of the police car, slotting into the lock
that clicked over his sister's wrists,
her hands so little—they slid out

So the soldier put the butt of his gun
to the back of her neck and his knee
on her back and chain around her wrist—
cinched it into a noose

The hole in their window refracted the flash
of fear in her eyes, the last time she blinked,
the glint of a north star stung his eyes as it
bounced from the edge of the steel binding
those thin hands—seared the last scene to memory,
arrested in flight, glistening blood in the matted black hair,
worried the police would catch his reflection

Over a wall, over the last crack,
tracing the last glint of a northern star,

to spend the next night and all other nights
in suspense, in the cool stone calm of a concrete desert
called San Jose slumped in the cupped hands of refuge,
the sanctuary of a church cellar

That first night, he forgot his name,
too tired to recall another one

(thankfully the same in English as in
his native tongue)

Click

The last night in his other country

Waiting for another siege,
watching through another broken-glass mosaic
reflection of the window,
remembering his first night after escaping home
to the first church that sheltered him
twenty years to the day

The same last night his sister closed her eyes
the last time, the same last sound heard
on the other side of the peeling wall

The click of the rusty lock opening

Could be father *Justo* or *La Migra*
Might as well be the executioner,
Might as well be Him, he prays,
come to call him back

Wrists tightened, too thick to bind him,
thick with his sister's pooling eyes,
swollen with his sister's tongue,
swelling with blood that flushes the floor

From his wrists?
From the slits of Mary's eyes?
Arrested in her last blink, the lids,
hands folded in a final rest

Hands that gathered, held him together
in the sanctuary on the first night,
now the last

As memory stretched home,
and the siren wailed from behind the wall
in the cool of the sanctuary, and the peace
of the chamber of a heart drained of terror
cast onto the other side, along with the frayed
prayer card, soft as his sister's hands, that told him

Prayer for Migrants:
To set off ... is to die a little
To arrive is never to arrive
until one is at rest with you
You, Lord, experienced migration
You brought it upon all men who know
what it is to live who seek
safe passage to the gates of heaven

The words that followed him
across the wall and back again,
one way or the other, he goes home tonight,
this last night like all the others
fleeing past him to the other side
of a day's journey, so close you can never tell
what side you are on

Through the glass that somehow
holds together—despite gravity,
best not to trust it, best to watch from
behind the cracks, best not to trust the moon
but trust the stars

On one side of the gate or the other,
in the crossing back to home,
whose name sounds the same
on any tongue in the midnight echo
of sanctuary

Mark

Before my mother
and grandmother
were a poem,
they rhymed

Before I dropped off
the period punctuating a stanza,
the verse was threaded
with stained strings running
through oblong spaces,
oxford commas,
pregnant silences

Women were versed before
they were encoded,
refracted in technologies of prose

They bled into vellum
they later brushed smooth
before wood pulp captured
the parched remains of discords,
of tradition

Every woman's birthright
a tether between bodies
to the bedpost, a measure of her distance
from her progeny and the proximity of an elder
before mothers were pedigrees
and scrolled stretch marks petrified in family trees

Grandmothers are poems nesting wisdom
before words swallow tongues,
lashing a belly button to remind you,
sliding across the body of her passage
that it's not a seal, a timestamp

or a maker's mark—but a scar,
a footnote born in the shape of a cross

Thank You

I would like to thank all the writing teachers I've had, broadly defined, especially anyone who has ever read my writing and told me they were confused by what it meant. Special thanks to Get Fresh, as well as Redbird Chapbooks and Anaphora Literary Press. And my deepest gratitude to all the characters and stories, real and imagined, that have peopled my poetry over the years, and have allowed me to capture a small snatch of their spirits on paper.

About the Poet

Michelle Chen is a writer and native New Yorker. "Point A to Point B" is her third chapbook, following "Baby Pepper" (Anaphora Literary Press) and "Postcards from Across the Street" (Redbird Chapbooks). She got her start in the literary world with her self-published zine in high school, and has since moved on to more conventional formats, as a contributing writer to *The Nation*, *Dissent*, *In These Times*, *The Washington Post, and The Guardian*. She also co-produces two podcasts on current events, Asia Pacific Forum and *Dissent*'s Belabored. Her journalistic writing focuses on immigration, labor, gender and other things that spark her outrage and imagination. She studied history at the City University of New York's Graduate Center, and still feels like she's not nearly well read enough.